Part #1
The Prophet

- In or about the year 570 the child who would be named Muhammad and who would become the Prophet of one of the world's great religions, Islam, was born into a family belonging to a clan of Quraish, the ruling tribe of Mecca, a city in the Hijaz region of northwestern Arabia.
- Originally the site of the Kaabah, a shrine of ancient origins, Mecca had, with the decline of southern Arabia, become an important center of sixth-century trade with such powers as the Sassanians, Byzantines, and Ethiopians. As a result, the city was dominated by powerful merchant families, among whom the men of Quraish were preeminent.

- Muhammad's father, 'Abd Allah ibn 'Abd al-Muttalib, died before the boy was born; his mother, Aminah, died when he was six. The orphan was entrusted to the care of his grandfather, the head of the clan of Hashim. After his grandfather's death, Muhammad was raised by his uncle, Abu Talib. As was customary, the young Muhammad was sent to live for a year or two with a Bedouin family. This practice, followed until recently by noble families of Mecca, Medina, Taif, and other towns of the Hijaz, had important implications for Muhammad.

- In addition to enduring the hardships of desert life, he acquired a taste for the rich language so cherished by the Arabs, whose speech was their proudest art. He also learned the patience and forbearance of the herdsmen, whose life of solitude he first shared and later came to understand and appreciate.

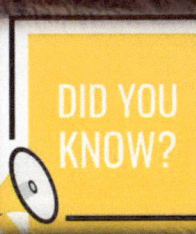

Did You Know?

- Around the year 590, Muhammad, then in his twenties, entered the service of a merchant widow named Khadijah as her agent, actively engaging in trading caravans to the north.

- Sometime later, he married her and had two sons, neither of whom survived, and four daughters.

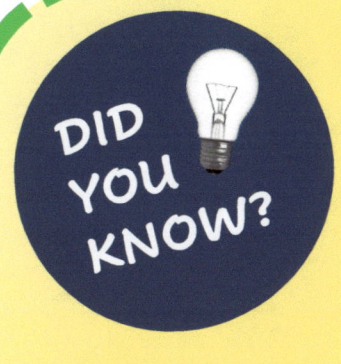

- In his forties, he began to retreat for meditation in a cave on Mount Hira, just outside Mecca, where the first of the great events of Islam took place. One day, as he was sitting in the cave, he heard a voice — later identified as that of the Angel Gabriel — which commanded him: "Recite in the name of your Lord who created — created man from a clot." (Qur'an 96:1–2)

- Three times Muhammad pleaded his inability to do so, but each time the command was repeated. Finally, he recited the words that are now the first five verses of the 96th chapter of the Qur'an — words that proclaim God as the Creator of man and the Source of all knowledge.

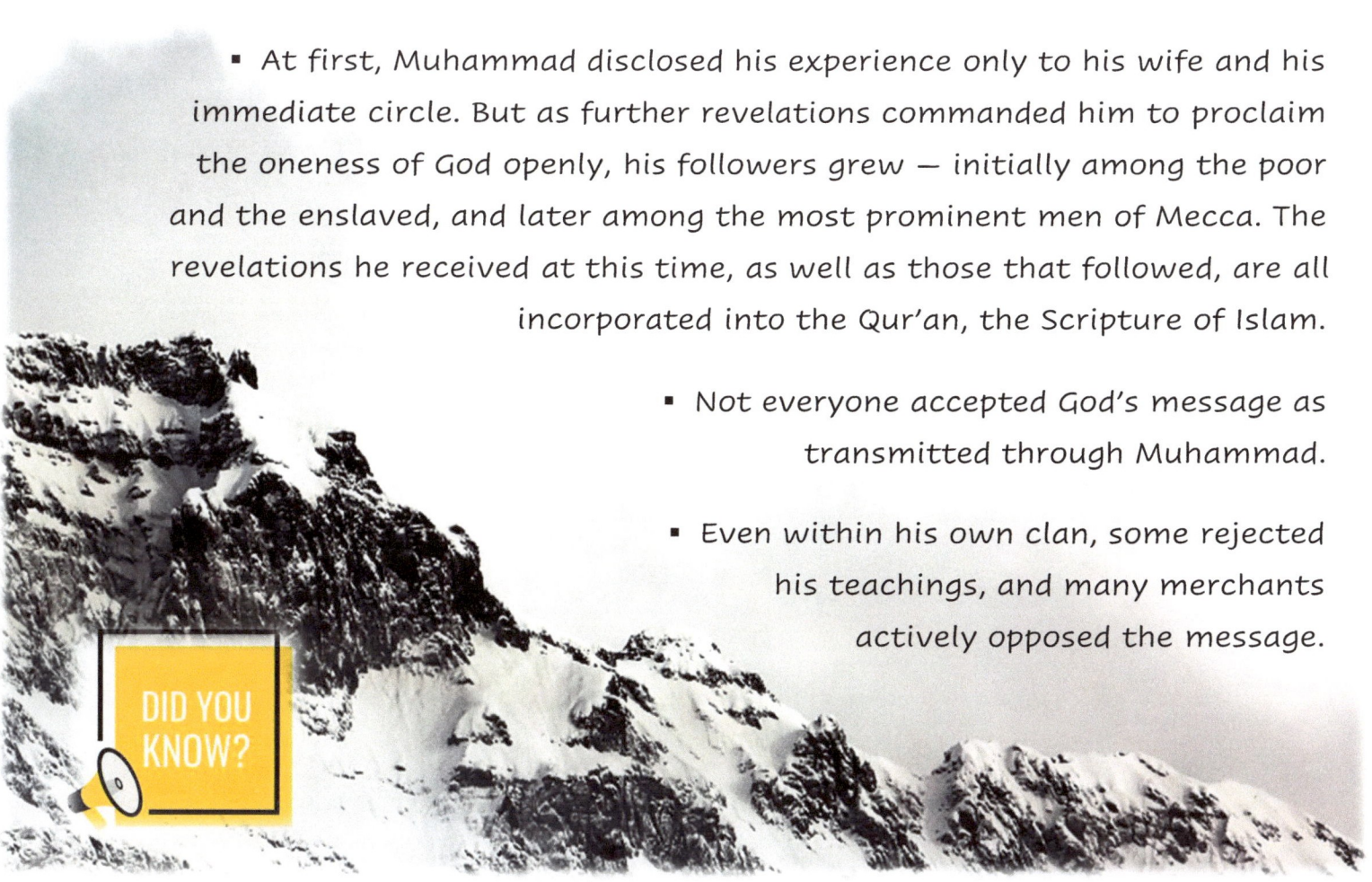

- At first, Muhammad disclosed his experience only to his wife and his immediate circle. But as further revelations commanded him to proclaim the oneness of God openly, his followers grew — initially among the poor and the enslaved, and later among the most prominent men of Mecca. The revelations he received at this time, as well as those that followed, are all incorporated into the Qur'an, the Scripture of Islam.

- Not everyone accepted God's message as transmitted through Muhammad.

- Even within his own clan, some rejected his teachings, and many merchants actively opposed the message.

DID YOU KNOW?

- The opposition, however, only served to sharpen Muhammad's sense of mission and deepen his understanding of how Islam differed from paganism. The belief in the Oneness of God was paramount in Islam; from this principle, all else follows. The verses of the Qur'an emphasize God's uniqueness, warn those who deny it of impending punishment, and proclaim His boundless compassion for those who submit to His will.
- They affirm the Last Judgment, when God, the Judge, will weigh the faith and deeds of each person, rewarding the faithful and punishing the transgressor. Because the Qur'an rejected polytheism and emphasized human moral responsibility, it presented a profound challenge to the worldly Meccans through powerful imagery.

- After Muhammad had preached publicly for more than a decade, opposition to him reached such intensity that, fearing for their safety, he sent some of his followers to Ethiopia. There, the Christian ruler granted them protection, the memory of which has been cherished by Muslims ever since. But in Mecca, the persecution worsened. Muhammad's followers were harassed, abused, and even tortured.
- At last, seventy of Muhammad's followers set off at his command to the northern town of Yathrib in the hope of establishing a new stage of the Islamic movement. This city was later renamed Medina ("The City"). In the early fall of 622, he, accompanied by his closest friend Abu Bakr al-Siddeeq, set out to join the emigrants. This event coincided with the leaders of Mecca plotting to kill him.

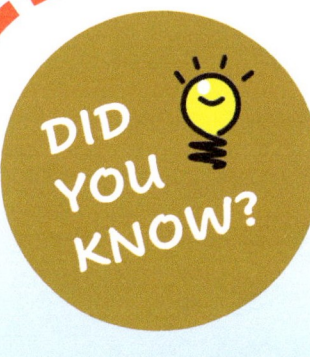

DID YOU KNOW?

- In Mecca, the plotters arrived at Muhammad's home only to find that his cousin, 'Ali, had taken his place in bed. Enraged, the Meccans placed a price on Muhammad's head and set out in pursuit. Muhammad and Abu Bakr, however, had taken refuge in a cave, where they hid from their pursuers.

- By the protection of God, the Meccans passed by the cave without noticing it, and Muhammad and Abu Bakr proceeded to Medina. There, they were joyfully welcomed by a throng of Medinans, as well as by the Meccans who had gone ahead to prepare the way. This was the Hijrah — anglicized as Hegira — usually, though inaccurately, translated as "Flight," from which the Muslim era is dated.

Did You Know?

- In fact, the Hijrah was not a flight, but a carefully planned migration that marked not only a break in history — the beginning of the Islamic era — but also, for Muhammad and the Muslims, a new way of life. Henceforth, the organizing principle of the community was no longer mere blood kinship, but the greater brotherhood of all Muslims. The men who accompanied Muhammad on the Hijrah were called the Muhajiroon — "those who made the Hijrah," or the "Emigrants" — while those in Medina who embraced Islam were called the Ansar, or "Helpers."

Did You Know?

- Muhammad was well acquainted with the situation in Medina. Earlier, before the Hijrah, some of its inhabitants had come to Mecca to perform the annual pilgrimage. As the Prophet would use this opportunity to call visiting pilgrims to Islam, the group from Medina heard his message and accepted it. They also invited Muhammad to settle in their city. After the Hijrah, Muhammad's exceptional qualities so impressed the Medinans that the rival tribes and their allies temporarily closed ranks. On March 15, 624, Muhammad and his supporters moved against the pagans of Mecca.

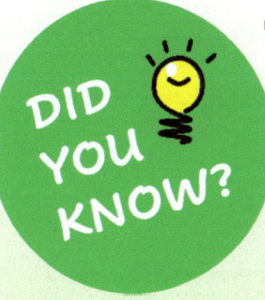

DID YOU KNOW?

- The first battle, which took place near Badr — now a small town southwest of Medina — had several important consequences. In the first place, the Muslim forces, though outnumbered three to one, routed the Meccans. Secondly, the discipline displayed by the Muslims brought home to the Meccans, perhaps for the first time, the capabilities of the man they had driven from their city.

- Thirdly, one of the allied tribes that had pledged support to the Muslims at the Battle of Badr, but proved lukewarm when the fighting began, was expelled from Medina one month after the battle. Those who claimed to be allies of the Muslims yet tacitly opposed them were thus served a warning: membership in the community imposed the obligation of full support.

- A year later, the Meccans struck back. Assembling an army of three thousand men, they met the Muslims at Uhud, a ridge outside Medina. After initial successes, the Muslims were driven back, and the Prophet himself was wounded. Although the Muslims were not completely defeated, the Meccans attacked Medina again two years later, this time with an army of ten thousand. At the Battle of the Trench, also known as the Battle of the Confederates, the Muslims achieved a decisive victory by introducing a new form of defense. On the side of Medina from which an attack was expected, they dug a trench too deep for the Meccan cavalry to cross without exposing themselves to the archers positioned behind earthworks on the city's side. After an inconclusive siege, the Meccans were forced to withdraw. Thereafter, Medina remained firmly in the hands of the Muslims.

Part #3
The Conquest

Did You Know?

- The Constitution of Medina — under which the clans accepting Muhammad as the Prophet of God formed an alliance, or federation — dates from this period. It demonstrated that the political consciousness of the Muslim community had reached an important stage; its members now defined themselves as a community distinct from all others. The Constitution also clarified the role of non-Muslims within the community. Jews, for example, were considered part of the community; they were dhimmis — that is, protected people — so long as they conformed to its laws.

Did You Know?

- This established a precedent for the treatment of subject peoples during the later conquests. Christians and Jews, upon payment of a nominal tax, were granted religious freedom and, while maintaining their status as non-Muslims, were considered associate members of the Muslim state. This status, however, did not apply to polytheists, who could not be accommodated within a community that worshipped the One God.

- It was around this time that Muhammad sent letters to the rulers of the world — the King of Persia, the Emperor of Byzantium, the Negus of Abyssinia, and the Governor of Egypt, among others — inviting them to submit to Islam.

- Nothing more fully illustrated the confidence of the small Muslim community, whose military power, despite the Battle of the Trench, remained negligible. Yet their confidence was not misplaced. Muhammad skillfully built a series of alliances among the tribes so that, by 628, he and fifteen hundred followers were able to demand access to the Kaaba. This was a milestone in Muslim history.
- Just a short time earlier, Muhammad had left the city of his birth to establish an Islamic state in Medina. Now, he was recognized by his former enemies as a leader in his own right. A year later, in 629, he reentered — and, in effect, conquered — Mecca without bloodshed and in a spirit of tolerance, establishing an ideal for future conquests. He also destroyed the idols in the Kaaba, putting an end once and for all to pagan practices there.

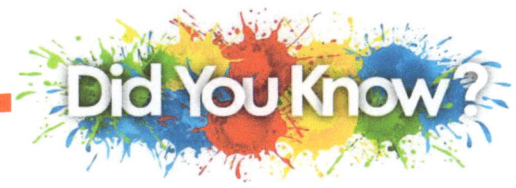

- At the same time, 'Amr ibn al-'As, the future conqueror of Egypt, and Khalid ibn al-Walid, the future "Sword of God," accepted Islam and swore allegiance to Muhammad. Their conversion was especially noteworthy, as these men had been among Muhammad's bitterest opponents only a short time before. In many ways, Muhammad's return to Mecca marked the climax of his mission. In 632, just three years later, he suddenly fell ill, and on June 8 of that year, with his third wife, Aisha, in attendance, the Messenger of God "died with the heat of noon."
- The death of Muhammad was a profound loss. To his followers, this simple man from Mecca was far more than a beloved friend, far more than a gifted administrator, and far more than the revered leader who had forged a new state from clusters of warring tribes.

- Muhammad was also the exemplar of the teachings he had brought from God: the teachings of the Qur'an, which for centuries have guided the thought, action, faith, and conduct of innumerable men and women, and which ushered in a distinctive era in the history of mankind. His death, however, had little effect on the dynamic society he had created in Arabia, and no effect at all on his central mission — to transmit the Qur'an to the world. As Abu Bakr famously said: "Whoever worshipped Muhammad should know that Muhammad is dead, but whoever worships God, then God is Ever-Living and shall never die."

Part #4
The Caliphate

Did You Know?

- With the death of Muhammad, the Muslim community was confronted with the question of succession: who would be its leader? Four individuals were widely regarded as the most suitable for leadership: Abu Bakr al-Siddeeq, who had not only accompanied Muhammad to Medina ten years earlier but had also been appointed to lead the public prayers during the Prophet's final illness; Umar ibn al-Khattab, a capable and trusted Companion of the Prophet; Uthman ibn 'Affan, a respected early convert; and 'Ali ibn Abi Talib, Muhammad's cousin and son-in-law.

Did You Know?

- Their piety and ability to govern the affairs of the Islamic nation were widely regarded as exemplary. At a meeting convened to decide the new leadership, Umar grasped Abu Bakr's hand and pledged his allegiance to him as a sign of recognition. By dusk, the community had reached consensus, and Abu Bakr was acknowledged as the Khalifah of Muhammad.

- Khalifah — anglicized as caliph — is a word meaning "successor," but it also suggests the nature of his historical role: to govern according to the Qur'an and the practice of the Prophet.

Did You Know?

- Abu Bakr's caliphate was short but significant. A capable leader, he lived simply, fulfilled his religious obligations assiduously, and remained accessible and sympathetic to his people. However, he also stood firm when some tribes, which had only nominally accepted Islam, renounced it in the wake of the Prophet's death.

- In a major accomplishment, Abu Bakr swiftly disciplined them. He then consolidated the support of the tribes within the Arabian Peninsula and directed their energies against the powerful empires of the East: the Sassanian Empire in Persia and the Byzantine Empire in Syria, Palestine, and Egypt. In short, he demonstrated the viability of the Muslim state.

- The second caliph, Umar — appointed by Abu Bakr — continued to demonstrate that viability. Adopting the title Ameer al-Mumineen, or Commander of the Believers, Umar extended Islam's temporal rule over Syria, Egypt, Iraq, and Persia in what were, from a purely military standpoint, astonishing victories.
- Within four years of the Prophet's death, the Muslim state had extended its sway over all of Syria and, at a famous battle fought during a sandstorm near the River Yarmuk, blunted the power of the Byzantines — whose ruler, Heraclius, had shortly before refused the call to accept Islam.
- Even more remarkably, the Muslim state administered the conquered territories with a tolerance almost unheard of in that age.

- At Damascus, for example, the Muslim leader Khalid ibn al-Walid signed a treaty that read as follows: "This is what Khalid ibn al-Walid grants to the inhabitants of Damascus upon entering it: he promises them security for their lives, property, and churches. Their city walls shall not be demolished, nor shall any Muslim be quartered in their houses. To this we give them the pact of God and the protection of His Prophet, the caliphs, and the believers. So long as they pay the poll tax, nothing but good shall befall them."

- This tolerance was characteristic of Islam. A year after Yarmuk, Umar, while in the military camp of al-Jabiyah on the Golan Heights, received word that the Byzantines were ready to surrender Jerusalem. Consequently, he rode there to accept the surrender in person. According to one account, he entered the city alone, clad in a simple cloak, astonishing a populace accustomed to the sumptuous garments and elaborate court ceremonials of the Byzantines and Persians.

Did You Know?

- He astounded them still further when he set their fears at rest by negotiating a generous treaty in which he assured them: "In the name of God... you have complete security for your churches, which shall not be occupied by the Muslims or destroyed." This policy proved successful everywhere. In Syria, for example, many Christians who had been involved in bitter theological disputes with the Byzantine authorities — and persecuted for them — welcomed the coming of Islam as an end to tyranny.

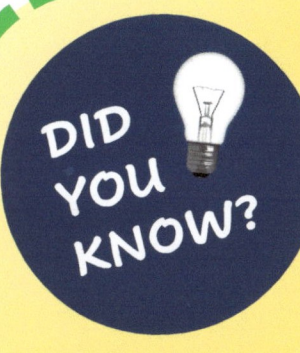

- In Egypt, which 'Amr ibn al-'As wrested from the Byzantines after a daring march across the Sinai Peninsula, the Coptic Christians not only welcomed the Arabs but also enthusiastically assisted them.

- This pattern was repeated throughout the Byzantine Empire. Conflicts among Greek Orthodox, Syrian Monophysites, Copts, and Nestorian Christians contributed to the failure of the Byzantines — always regarded as intruders — to gain popular support, while the tolerance shown by Muslims toward Christians and Jews removed the primary cause for opposition.

Did You Know?

- Umar adopted this approach in administrative matters as well. Although he appointed Muslim governors to the new provinces, existing Byzantine and Persian bureaucracies were retained wherever possible. For fifty years, Greek remained the chancery language of Syria, Egypt, and Palestine, while Pahlavi, the chancery language of the Sassanian Empire, continued to be used in Mesopotamia and Persia. Umar, who served as caliph for ten years, concluded his rule with a significant victory over the Persian Empire.

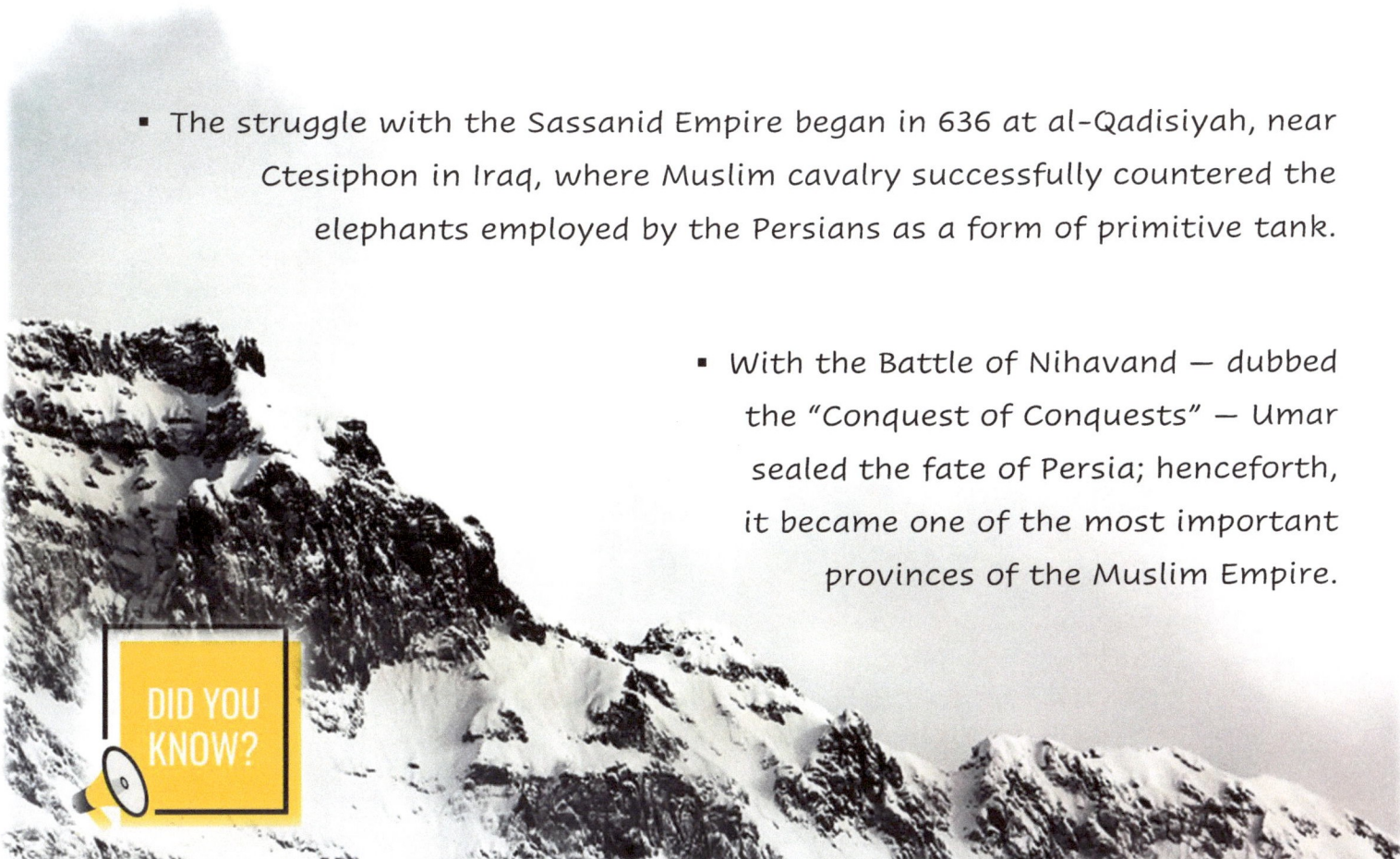

- The struggle with the Sassanid Empire began in 636 at al-Qadisiyah, near Ctesiphon in Iraq, where Muslim cavalry successfully countered the elephants employed by the Persians as a form of primitive tank.

- With the Battle of Nihavand — dubbed the "Conquest of Conquests" — Umar sealed the fate of Persia; henceforth, it became one of the most important provinces of the Muslim Empire.

DID YOU KNOW?

Did You Know?

- His caliphate marked a high point in early Islamic history. He was renowned for his justice, social vision, administrative skill, and statesmanship.

- His innovations left a lasting imprint on social welfare, taxation, and the financial and administrative framework of the expanding empire.

Part #5
The Caliphate (Uthman)

Did You Know?

- Umar ibn al-Khattab, the second caliph of Islam, was stabbed while leading the Fajr prayer by Abu Lu'lu'ah, a Persian Magian slave. As Umar lay on his deathbed, those around him asked him to appoint a successor. Instead, Umar appointed a committee of six men to choose the next caliph from among themselves.

- This committee comprised 'Ali ibn Abi Talib, 'Uthman ibn 'Affan, 'Abd al-Rahman ibn 'Awf, Sa'd ibn Abi Waqqas, al-Zubayr ibn al-'Awwam, and Talhah ibn 'Ubayd Allah, who were among the most eminent Companions of the Prophet.

- Umar instructed that the Election Committee should choose a successor within three days, and that the new caliph should assume office on the fourth day. As two days passed without a decision, the members grew anxious, sensing that time was running out and that no solution was yet in sight. 'Abd al-Rahman ibn 'Awf then offered to withdraw his own candidacy if the others agreed to abide by his decision. They consented, entrusting him with the selection of the next caliph. He consulted each nominee and went throughout Medina seeking the views of the people. Ultimately, he selected 'Uthman as the new caliph, as the majority favored him.

Did You Know?

- 'Uthman led a simple life even after becoming the leader of the Islamic state. It would have been easy for a successful businessman like him to live in luxury, but he never sought such a life in this world. His only aim was to attain the pleasure of the Hereafter, as he understood that this world is merely a temporary test. 'Uthman's generosity continued even after he became caliph.

Did You Know?

- The caliphs were compensated for their services from the treasury, but 'Uthman never accepted any salary for his service to Islam. Moreover, he established the practice of freeing slaves every Friday, caring for widows and orphans, and giving generously in charity. His patience and endurance were among the qualities that contributed to his success as a leader.

- 'Uthman achieved much during his reign. He pressed forward with the pacification of Persia, continued to defend the Muslim state against the Byzantines, incorporated what is now Libya into the empire, and brought much of Armenia under Muslim rule. 'Uthman also, through his cousin Mu'awiyah ibn Abi Sufyan, the governor of Syria, established an Arab navy that fought a series of significant engagements against the Byzantines.
- Of even greater importance to Islam, however, was 'Uthman's compilation of the text of the Qur'an as revealed to the Prophet. Realizing that the original message might be inadvertently affected by textual variations, he appointed a committee to compile the authorized recension and eliminate variant copies. The result was the text that has been accepted throughout the Muslim world to this day.

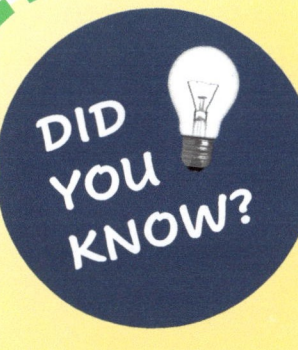

- During his caliphate, 'Uthman faced considerable hostility from newly converted, nominal Muslims in recently incorporated Islamic lands, who began to accuse him of not following the example of the Prophet and the preceding caliphs in matters of governance. However, the Companions of the Prophet consistently defended him. These accusations did not alter his conduct.

- He remained steadfast in his determination to be a merciful leader. Even when his opponents turned against him, he did not use funds from the treasury to protect his house or himself. As foretold by the Prophet Muhammad, 'Uthman's enemies relentlessly sought to undermine his authority by constantly opposing and accusing him. Eventually, they plotted against him, surrounded his house, and incited others to kill him.

Did You Know?

- Many of his advisors urged him to resist the assault, but he refused, until he was killed while reciting the Qur'an, just as the Prophet had foretold. 'Uthman died as a martyr. Anas ibn Malik narrated the following: "The Prophet once climbed Mount Uhud with Abu Bakr, 'Umar, and 'Uthman. The mountain shook beneath them. The Prophet said (to the mountain), 'Be firm, O Uhud! For upon you stand a Prophet, a truthful supporter, and two martyrs.'"
  - (Sahih al-Bukhari)

EXTRA BONUS

A

- Allah: The name Muslims use for God, who made everything.
- Akhlaq: Being kind, polite, and good to everyone.
- Ablution (Wudu): Washing hands, face, and feet before praying.
- Adhan: A call to prayer to tell everyone it's time to pray.
- Alhamdulillah: Saying "Thank you, Allah!" for all the blessings He gives us.
- Al-Quran: The holy book of Islam, which teaches us how to live a good life.
- Amal: Doing good actions that make Allah happy.
- Ameen: A word we say at the end of a dua, meaning "Please accept it, Allah!"
- Angels (Malaikah): Special beings made by Allah to do His work, like bringing messages or protecting us.
- Arafah: A special day during Hajj when pilgrims pray on a big plain.
- Ar-Rahman: One of Allah's names, meaning "The Most Merciful."
- Ar-Raheem: Another name of Allah, meaning "The Most Kind."
- Ashura: A special day in the Islamic calendar when we remember important events.

- Ayah: A verse in the Quran that teaches us something about Allah and life.
- Aqidah: Believing in Allah and His teachings as the foundation of our faith.

B

- Bismillah: It means "In the name of Allah," said before starting anything good.
- Barakah: Special blessings and goodness from Allah.
- Burqa: A piece of clothing some Muslim women wear to cover themselves.
- Bab-ul-Rahmah: The Gate of Mercy in a mosque, like a special door.
- Bilal: A companion of Prophet Muhammad (peace be upon him) and the first person to call the Adhan.
- Badr: The name of an important battle where Muslims prayed to Allah for help and won with His support.
- Baitullah: Another name for the Kaaba, meaning "The House of Allah."

- Bukhari: A famous collection of Hadith (sayings of Prophet Muhammad, peace be upon him).
- Baraqah (Buraq): A special creature that carried Prophet Muhammad (peace be upon him) on his night journey to the heavens.
- Bay'ah: A promise made by people to follow and obey their leader in Islam.
- Birr: Being good and kind, especially to your parents.
- Burhan: Clear evidence or proof, like the Quran, that shows Allah's truth.
- Baqi: A famous graveyard in Madinah where many of the Prophet's companions are buried.
- Bismillah-ir-Rahman-ir-Raheem: The full phrase meaning "In the name of Allah, the Most Merciful, the Most Kind," often said at the start of the Quran's chapters.
- Bayan: A speech or talk given to explain Islamic teachings and inspire people.

C

- Caliph: A leader who helps guide the Muslim community.
- Charity (Sadaqah): Giving to people in need to make them happy.
- Camel: An animal important in Islamic history, often used in desert journeys.
- Companions (Sahabah): Friends of Prophet Muhammad (peace be upon him).

Here's an expanded list of 11 more terminologies under C with simple explanations suitable for children:

- Cave of Hira: The special place where Prophet Muhammad (peace be upon him) first received Allah's message.
- Creation: Everything Allah made, like people, animals, trees, and stars.
- Crescent: A curved moon shape that is often seen on mosques and used to start Islamic months.
- Commandments: Important rules from Allah that teach us how to live a good life.
- Community (Ummah): All Muslims around the world who follow Islam.
- Clarity: The feeling of understanding when Allah helps us know what's right.
- Comfort: The peace we feel when we trust Allah to take care of us.

- Compassion: Caring for others just like Allah cares for us.
- Cleanliness: Staying clean and pure, which is very important in Islam.
- Converts: People who choose to follow Islam later in their lives.
- Celebration: Happy times like Eid when Muslims come together to pray, eat, and share joy.

D

- Dua: Talking to Allah and asking for help or saying thank you.
- Deen: A word that means religion or way of life in Islam.
- Dawood (David): A prophet who loved to sing and praised Allah.
- Dhikr: Remembering Allah by saying words like "SubhanAllah" (Glory to Allah).
- Dua: Talking to Allah and asking for help or saying thank you.
- Deen: A word that means religion or way of life in Islam.
- Dawood (David): A prophet who loved to sing and praised Allah.
- Dhikr: Remembering Allah by saying words like "SubhanAllah" (Glory to Allah).
- Darul Aman: A place of peace and safety.
- Dawah: Inviting others to learn about and understand Islam.

- Dajjal: A deceiver mentioned in Islamic eschatology who will appear before the Day of Judgment.
- Darul Harb: Lands not governed by Islamic law, often referred to as territories of conflict.
- Darul Islam: Lands governed by Islamic law, promoting peace and justice.
- Dirham: A silver coin used as currency in early Islamic history.
- Dhul-Hijjah: The twelfth and final month of the Islamic lunar calendar, in which Hajj takes place.
- Dhul-Qarnayn: A figure mentioned in the Quran known for his just rule and building barriers to protect people from harm.
- Dunya: Refers to this world and its temporary nature compared to the eternal Hereafter.

E

- Eid: A happy celebration after Ramadan or Hajj, with prayers, sweets, and gifts.
- Eman (Iman): Believing in Allah and His teachings with your heart.
- Ehsan: Being extra kind and doing your best in everything.
- Eidgah: A big open place where Muslims pray together on Eid.
- Eid: A happy celebration after Ramadan or Hajj, with prayers, sweets, and gifts.
- Eman (Iman): Believing in Allah and His teachings with your heart.
- Ehsan: Being extra kind and doing your best in everything.
- Eidgah: A big open place where Muslims pray together on Eid.
- Eid ul-Fitr: The festival marking the end of Ramadan, celebrated with joy and charity.

- Eid ul-Adha: The festival of sacrifice, remembering Prophet Ibrahim's obedience to Allah.
- Ebadah (Ibadah): Acts of worship like praying, fasting, and being good to others.
- Eblis: Another name for Shaytan (Satan), who disobeyed Allah.
- Eeman (Faith): A strong belief in Allah, His angels, books, prophets, the Day of Judgment, and destiny.
- Ehtikaf (Itikaf): Staying in the mosque for worship, especially during the last ten days of Ramadan.
- Ehsanul Khaliqeen: A name of Allah meaning "The Best of Creators."
- Eid Mubarak: A greeting exchanged during Eid, meaning "Blessed Eid."
- Eid Salat: The special prayer offered on the morning of Eid.

F

- Fajr: The first prayer of the day, done at dawn.
- Fasting (Sawm): Not eating or drinking from dawn to sunset in Ramadan.
- Fard: Something Allah tells us we must do, like praying five times a day.
- Fiqh: Rules that help us understand what is right and wrong in Islam.
- Fatiha: The first chapter of the Quran, recited in every unit of prayer.
- Faith (Iman): Believing in Allah, His angels, His books, His messengers, the Last Day, and destiny.
- Fitnah: A trial or test that challenges faith or causes trouble.
- Fidyah: Compensation given for missing a fast, such as feeding the poor.
- Fitrah: The natural disposition or state humans are born with, inclined toward worshiping Allah.
- Fard Kifayah: A communal obligation, like attending a funeral prayer, where some members of the community fulfill it on behalf of others.
- Furqan: Another name for the Quran, meaning "the criterion" that distinguishes right from wrong.
- Fajr Sunnah: The two recommended units of prayer before the obligatory Fajr prayer.

- Fiqh-ul-Ibadat: The study of rules related to worship, such as prayer, fasting, and pilgrimage.
- Farah: A state of joy and happiness that pleases Allah.
- Fuqaha: Scholars who are experts in Islamic jurisprudence (Fiqh).

G

- Gabriel (Jibreel): An angel who brought Allah's messages to prophets.
- Ghusl: A special bath to clean yourself before praying or after certain events.
- Grateful (Shukr): Saying thank you to Allah for everything He gives us.
- Guidance: Help from Allah to do what is right and stay on the good path.
- Gabriel (Jibreel): An angel who brought Allah's messages to prophets.
- Ghusl: A special bath to clean yourself before praying or after certain events.
- Grateful (Shukr): Saying thank you to Allah for everything He gives us.
- Guidance: Help from Allah to do what is right and stay on the good path.
- Ghafir: One of Allah's names, meaning "The Forgiving."
- Ghadab: The word for anger in Arabic, which believers are encouraged to control.

- Garden (Jannah): The beautiful place of paradise Allah promises to the good.
- Good Deeds (A'mal Salih): Actions that please Allah, like helping others and being kind.
- Generosity: Sharing what you have with others for the sake of Allah.
- Ghaib: Things that are unseen, like angels and the Day of Judgment, which we believe in through faith.
- Golden Rule: Treating others the way you want to be treated, as taught in Islam.
- Grave (Qabr): The place where a person is buried and where the journey to the Hereafter begins.
- Ghaffar: Another name of Allah, meaning "The Oft-Forgiving."

H

- Hajj: A special trip to the Kaaba in Makkah that Muslims make once in their life if they can.
- Halal: Things that are allowed for Muslims, like certain foods.
- Haram: Things that are not allowed in Islam, like lying or stealing.
- Hijab: A scarf some Muslim women wear to cover their hair.
- Hijrah: The journey Prophet Muhammad (peace be upon him) took from Makkah to Madinah.
- Hadith: The sayings and actions of Prophet Muhammad (peace be upon him) that teach Muslims how to live.
- Hafiz: A person who has memorized the entire Quran.
- Halq: The shaving of the head, often done after completing Hajj or Umrah.
- Hamzah: One of Prophet Muhammad's (peace be upon him) uncles who was known for his bravery and became a martyr.
- Haneef: Someone who follows the pure monotheistic way of worshipping Allah.
- Haram (Sanctuary): A sacred area, like the Masjid al-Haram in Makkah or Masjid an-Nabawi in Madinah.
- Hasanat: Good deeds that earn rewards from Allah.

- Hudhud: The hoopoe bird mentioned in the Quran in the story of Prophet Sulaiman (Solomon).
- Hudood: The limits set by Allah, such as laws for society and worship.
- Hikmah: Wisdom or understanding given by Allah.
- Houri: Beautiful beings mentioned in the Quran as a reward in Paradise.

I

- Islam: The religion of peace and submission to Allah.
- Ihsan: Doing good deeds in the best way possible, with love for Allah.
- Iftar: The meal Muslims eat to break their fast in Ramadan.
- Imam: A leader who guides the prayer in a mosque.
- InshaAllah: It means "If Allah wills," said when planning something.
- Ibadah: Acts of worship performed to please Allah, such as prayer and fasting.
- Ilm: Knowledge or the pursuit of learning, highly valued in Islam.
- Ikhlas: Sincerity and purity of intention in worship and actions.
- Israa: The miraculous night journey of Prophet Muhammad (PBUH) from Mecca to Jerusalem.

- Iblis: The name of Satan, who disobeyed Allah and was cast out of Heaven.
- Ijma: Consensus or agreement among Islamic scholars on religious matters.
- Ihsan: Excellence in worship and character, striving for perfection in actions.
- Iqra: The first word revealed to Prophet Muhammad (PBUH), meaning "Read."
- Iddah: The waiting period a woman observes after divorce or the death of her husband.
- Ismail (Ishmael): A prophet, the son of Ibrahim (Abraham), known for his patience and obedience.
- Imaan: Faith or belief in Allah, His prophets, and His teachings.

J

- Jannah: Paradise, the beautiful garden where good people go after they die.
- Jinn: Invisible beings created by Allah from smokeless fire.
- Jumu'ah: The special prayer on Friday for Muslims.
- Justice (Adl): Being fair and treating everyone kindly.
- Jibreel (Gabriel): The angel who brought Allah's messages to the prophets.
- Jahannam: Hell, a place for those who do not follow Allah's guidance.
- Jam'ah: A group prayer performed together.
- Janazah: The Islamic funeral prayer for the deceased.

- Juz: One of the 30 parts of the Quran for easier reading and memorization.
- Jaiz: Something allowed or permissible in Islam.
- Jihad: Striving or struggling for a good cause, especially to live according to Allah's guidance.
- Jilbab: A long, loose-fitting coat or outer garment worn by some Muslim women.
- Jadid: A term meaning "new" or "fresh" in Arabic.
- Jamrah: A pillar representing Satan that Muslims throw stones at during Hajj.
- Jabbar: One of Allah's names, meaning "The Compeller" or "The All-Powerful."

K

- Kaaba: The black cube in Makkah that Muslims pray towards.
- Khalifa: A person chosen to take care of Allah's creations and lead with goodness.
- Kindness: Being nice and caring for people, animals, and nature.
- Kiswa: The black cloth that covers the Kaaba.
- Kaaba: The black cube in Makkah that Muslims pray towards.
- Khalifa: A person chosen to take care of Allah's creations and lead with goodness.
- Kindness: Being nice and caring for people, animals, and nature.
- Kiswa: The black cloth that covers the Kaaba.
- Kalima: A declaration of faith in Islam, meaning "There is no god but Allah, and Muhammad is His Messenger."
- Khutbah: A sermon or speech, especially the one given during the Friday prayer (Jumu'ah).

- Kaba'il: Tribes or groups of people in Arab culture.
- Khair: Goodness or blessings.
- Kufr: Denial or disbelief in Allah.
- Kanz: Treasure or something precious.
- Kitab: Book, often referring to the holy books revealed by Allah.
- Karim: Generous or noble, one of Allah's attributes (Al-Karim).
- Khalil: Close friend, often used to refer to Prophet Ibrahim as "Khalilullah" (Friend of Allah).

L

- Lailatul Qadr: A special night in Ramadan when prayers are extra powerful.
- Love: Caring deeply for Allah, family, friends, and all His creations.
- Luqman: A wise man mentioned in the Quran who gave good advice to his son.
- Learning (Ilm): Gaining knowledge to understand the world and become closer to Allah.
- Lailatul Qadr: A special night in Ramadan when prayers are extra powerful.
- Love: Caring deeply for Allah, family, friends, and all His creations.
- Luqman: A wise man mentioned in the Quran who gave good advice to his son.
- Learning (Ilm): Gaining knowledge to understand the world and become closer to Allah.

- Lutf (Kindness): Allah's gentle care and mercy toward His creations.
- Lisan (Tongue): The part of the body used for speaking, which should always say good words.
- Labbayk: A word meaning "I am here," often said during Hajj to respond to Allah's call.
- Lillah: Something done purely for the sake of Allah.
- Lantern (Fanous): A traditional decorative light, often used during Ramadan.
- Loyalty: Being faithful and committed to Allah and His teachings.
- Layyin (Softness): Being gentle and soft in speech and behavior, as taught in Islam.
- Light (Noor): A symbol of guidance and purity, often associated with Allah's guidance.
- Lament: Feeling regret or sorrow, turning to Allah for forgiveness.

M

- Makkah: The holiest city for Muslims where the Kaaba is located.
- Masjid: Another word for mosque, a place where Muslims pray.
- Mercy (Rahma): Allah's kindness and forgiveness for everyone.
- Madinah: The city where Prophet Muhammad (peace be upon him) is buried.
- Minaret: The tall tower of a mosque from where the call to prayer is made.
- Mihrab: A niche in the wall of a mosque that indicates the direction of the Kaaba in Makkah (Qibla), toward which Muslims pray.
- Minbar: A pulpit in the mosque where the imam delivers the Friday sermon (Khutbah).
- Muezzin: The person who calls Muslims to prayer from the minaret of a mosque.

- Mahr: A mandatory gift or dowry given by the groom to the bride in Islamic marriage.
- Mufti: An Islamic scholar qualified to issue legal opinions or fatwas.
- Mujahid: A person engaged in jihad, striving or struggling in the way of Allah.
- Mahram: A close relative with whom marriage is forbidden, providing a lawful level of interaction.
- Mukallaf: A person who is legally responsible in Islamic law, having reached maturity and sanity.
- Mubah: Actions in Islam that are permissible and neither rewarded nor punished.
- Mushaf: A physical copy of the Qur'an.
- Masjid al-Haram: The Sacred Mosque in Makkah, encompassing the Kaaba and the holiest site in Islam.

N

- Nabi: A prophet chosen by Allah to guide people.
- Nafs: Our inner self that sometimes needs to be taught patience.
- Nikah: A marriage ceremony in Islam.

- Noor: Light, often used to describe Allah's guidance or blessings.
- Nasihah: Sincere advice or guidance given for the benefit of others.
- Niyyah: Intention, a key aspect in Islam as actions are judged by their intentions.
- Nasr: Help or victory granted by Allah.
- Nabi-ul-Ummi: A title of Prophet Muhammad (peace be upon him), meaning "The Unlettered Prophet."
- Nafs-e-Mutmainnah: The contented soul, one at peace with Allah's will.
- Nifaq: Hypocrisy, considered a severe spiritual ailment in Islam.
- Nawafil: Voluntary prayers or acts of worship beyond the obligatory ones.

- Nahr: Ritual animal sacrifice performed during Eid-ul-Adha.
- Nur-ul-Quran: The light and guidance derived from the Quran.
- Nuzul: The descent or revelation of the Quran upon the Prophet Muhammad (peace be upon him).
- Nasab: Lineage or ancestry, often emphasized in Islamic family and inheritance laws.

O

- Obedience: Listening to Allah and following His commands with love.
- Omar (Umar): A wise and strong companion of the Prophet Muhammad (peace be upon him).
- Offering (Sadaqah): Giving money or help to people in need to make them happy.
- Ottoman: A Muslim empire that ruled many lands long ago.
- Obligation (Fard): A required act in Islam that must be performed by every Muslim.
- Oneness (Tawheed): The belief in the unity and singularity of Allah, central to Islamic faith.
- Oasis: A fertile spot in the desert, often mentioned in Islamic history and geography.
- Orphans (Yatama): Children without parents, who hold a special place in Islam and are to be treated with care and compassion.
- Omar ibn Abdul Aziz: A revered Umayyad caliph known for his justice and piety.

- Oaths (Ayman): Swearing by Allah in serious matters, with emphasis on truthfulness.
- Oppression (Zulm): Any form of injustice or wrongdoing, strongly condemned in Islam.
- Oblation (Qurbani): The act of sacrificing an animal during Eid al-Adha to honor Prophet Ibrahim's devotion.
- Obedient Angels: Angels who fulfill Allah's commands without question or disobedience.
- Ordeal (Ibtilaa): A test or trial given by Allah to strengthen faith and patience.
- Olive (Zaytoon): A blessed fruit mentioned in the Qur'an, symbolizing purity and goodness.

P

- Prophet: A person Allah chose to teach people the right way, like Prophet Muhammad (peace be upon him).
- Patience (Sabr): Staying calm and trusting Allah during hard times.
- Prayer (Salah): Talking to Allah five times a day.
- Peace (Salaam): Being calm and kind to everyone around you.
- Paradise (Jannah): The eternal home of happiness and reward for those who follow Allah's guidance.
- Piety (Taqwa): Being mindful of Allah in all actions and decisions.
- Prostration (Sujood): Bowing down in humility and worship during Salah.

- Prophethood (Nubuwwah): The responsibility given by Allah to chosen individuals to guide humanity.

- Purity (Tahara): Staying clean in body, mind, and soul as part of faith.
- Pilgrimage (Hajj): A journey to Makkah required once in a lifetime for those who are able.
- Poverty (Faqr): A state that is not a punishment but a test and opportunity for gratitude and patience.
- People of the Book (Ahlul Kitab): Refers to Jews and Christians who received earlier scriptures.
- Punishment (Azaab): The consequence of disobedience to Allah, in this life or the Hereafter.
- Prophetic Traditions (Hadith): The sayings, actions, and approvals of Prophet Muhammad (peace be upon him).
- Promise (Wa'd): A commitment that must be fulfilled, reflecting honesty and trustworthiness.

Q

- Quran: The holy book of Islam, full of Allah's words.

- Qibla: The direction Muslims face when they pray, towards the Kaaba.
- Qadr (Destiny): Knowing that Allah has a plan for everything.
- Qunut: A special prayer said during some salahs.
- Quraysh: The prominent tribe of Makkah to which Prophet Muhammad (PBUH) belonged.
- Qisas: The principle of retributive justice in Islamic law.
- Qurban: The act of sacrificing an animal for Allah, especially during Eid al-Adha.
- Qalam: The "pen" used metaphorically in the Quran, representing knowledge and wisdom.
- Qari: A person who recites the Quran with proper tajweed and melodious tone.

- Qudsi Hadith: Sacred narrations where Allah's words are conveyed through the Prophet (PBUH), but not part of the Quran.
- Qayamat (Day of Judgment): The day when all souls will be resurrected for accountability.
- Qawwam: A term referring to the role of men as maintainers or protectors of women in the family.
- Qanun: Laws or regulations derived from Islamic principles.
- Qabr: The grave where a person is buried after death.
- Qalb: The heart, often referred to in Islamic teachings as the spiritual center of a person.

R

- Ramadan: The holy month when Muslims fast and do good deeds.
- Rahman: A name of Allah meaning "The Most Merciful."
- Respect: Treating everyone nicely because Allah loves kind people.
- Ruqyah: Prayers said to ask Allah for healing and protection.
- Rabi' al-Awwal: The third month in the Islamic calendar, known for the birth of Prophet Muhammad (PBUH).
- Raheem: A name of Allah meaning "The Most Compassionate."
- Raka'ah: A unit of prayer in Salah (Islamic prayer).
- Rajab: The seventh month in the Islamic calendar, considered one of the sacred months.
- Rizq: Sustenance or provision provided by Allah.

- Righteousness: Acting in a way that pleases Allah and aligns with His commands.
- Rahmah: Mercy or compassion, a key characteristic encouraged in Islam.
- Rumi: A famous Islamic poet and scholar known for his spiritual writings.
- Ruh: The soul or spirit, considered the essence of life.
- Ramadan Kareem: A common greeting during Ramadan meaning "Generous Ramadan."
- Rowdah: The sacred area in the Prophet's Mosque in Medina, often referred to as a garden of Paradise.

S

- Salah: The five daily prayers that Muslims do.
- Sawm: Fasting during Ramadan, where Muslims don't eat or drink from dawn to sunset.
- Shahada: The statement of belief: "There is no god but Allah, and Muhammad is His messenger."
- Shukr: Being thankful to Allah for all the blessings He gives.
- Sadaqah: Voluntary charity given to help others and earn Allah's pleasure.
- Sajdah: The act of prostration during prayer, showing humility before Allah.

- Sharia: The divine law derived from the Quran and Sunnah, guiding all aspects of a Muslim's life.
- Shirk: Associating partners with Allah, considered the gravest sin in Islam.

- SubhanAllah: An expression meaning "Glory be to Allah," used to praise His perfection.
- Sunnah: The teachings, actions, and sayings of Prophet Muhammad (PBUH).
- Surah: A chapter of the Quran; there are 114 Surahs in the Quran.
- Sidq: Truthfulness and honesty in words and actions.
- Sirat al-Mustaqeem: The Straight Path; the way of living that pleases Allah.
- Sabr: Patience and perseverance in the face of difficulties.
- Salam: Peace; often used as a greeting in the phrase "As-salamu alaykum" meaning "Peace be upon you."

T

- Taqwa: Being aware of Allah and trying to do what He loves.
- Tawheed: Believing in only one God, Allah.
- Tahajjud: A special prayer done at night, when everyone else is asleep.
- Tasbeeh: Saying words of praise like "SubhanAllah" (Glory to Allah) many times.
- Tafseer: The explanation or interpretation of the Quran.
- Taharah: The state of cleanliness or purity in Islam, often achieved through wudu (ablution) or ghusl (ritual bath).
- Takaful: Islamic mutual insurance based on shared responsibility and cooperation.
- Taqdeer: The concept of divine destiny or predestination in Islam.
- Tawaaf: The act of circling the Kaaba during Hajj or Umrah as a form of worship.

- Tawakkul: Placing complete trust and reliance on Allah while taking appropriate actions.
- Takbeer: The declaration "Allahu Akbar" (Allah is the Greatest), often said in prayers and other acts of worship.
- Tarawih: Special prayers performed in congregation during the nights of Ramadan.
- Tahneek: A Sunnah practice of softening a date and rubbing it on a newborn's palate.
- Talbiyah: A supplication made by pilgrims during Hajj or Umrah, beginning with "Labbayk Allahumma Labbayk."
- Tafakkur: Reflecting and pondering on the signs of Allah in the universe and creation.

u

- Umrah: A smaller pilgrimage to Makkah that Muslims can do anytime.
- Umar: A strong and wise companion of Prophet Muhammad (peace be upon him).
- Unity: Muslims coming together to help and care for each other.
- Udhiyah: Sacrificing an animal like a sheep during Eid-ul-Adha to remember Prophet Ibrahim's (Abraham's) story.
- Usrah: A small group gathering of Muslims for learning and sharing Islamic knowledge.

- Ulul-Azm: Refers to the five greatest Prophets: Noah, Abraham, Moses, Jesus, and Muhammad (peace be upon them all).
- Ulama: Islamic scholars who have deep knowledge of Islamic teachings and jurisprudence.

- Usul al-Fiqh: Principles of Islamic jurisprudence used to derive rulings from the Quran and Sunnah.
- Ummah: The global Muslim community united by faith and principles.
- Udhun: Refers to the ear, often mentioned in the context of listening and obedience in Islamic teachings.
- Urdu: A widely spoken language among Muslims, with many Islamic texts and poetry written in it.
- Udhiyyah: The act of animal sacrifice during Eid-ul-Adha in remembrance of Prophet Ibrahim's devotion to Allah.
- Ummi: A term referring to the Prophet Muhammad (peace be upon him) as being unlettered or not formally taught to read and write.
- Uquq al-Walidain: The sin of disobedience or mistreatment towards one's parents.
- Ufuq: The horizon, often mentioned in the Quran in the context of Allah's signs in creation.

V

- Victory (Nasr): Success that comes with Allah's help.
- Virtue: Doing something good and pleasing to Allah.
- Verse (Ayah): A sentence in the Quran that teaches us something important.

- Values: Special rules like being honest, kind, and fair, taught by Islam.
- Vow (Nadhr): A solemn promise made to Allah to perform a specific act of worship or good deed if a wish is fulfilled.
- Volition (Ikhtiyar): The ability to make choices and decisions freely as granted by Allah.
- Validity (Sihhah): The state of an act or worship being correct and acceptable in accordance with Islamic law.
- Verification (Tathabut): The process of confirming or authenticating information before accepting it as true, as taught in Islam.

- Virtuous Deeds (A'mal Salihah): Actions performed sincerely for the sake of Allah, in accordance with His commands.
- Veneration (Tafdhil): Deep respect and honor for something or someone, such as the Prophets or the Quran.
- Visions (Ru'ya): Dreams or sights that may hold spiritual significance, sometimes viewed as guidance or warnings.
- Vindication (Tazkiyah): The act of clearing someone from blame or sin, often linked to personal purification.
- Vigilance (Muraqabah): Awareness and mindfulness of Allah's constant presence and observation.
- Visitor (Zair): Someone who visits sacred sites, such as the Kaaba or the graves of Prophets, with reverence and respect.
- Voluntary Acts (Nawafil): Optional deeds or acts of worship performed beyond the obligatory ones to earn extra rewards.

W

- Wudu: Washing parts of the body to be clean before praying.

- Wisdom (Hikmah): Using knowledge in the best way to make good choices.
- Wa Alaikum Salaam: The reply to "As-salaamu Alaikum," meaning "Peace be upon you too."
- Wahy: Messages from Allah given to prophets through angels like Jibreel (Gabriel).
- Wudu: Washing parts of the body to be clean before praying.
- Wisdom (Hikmah): Using knowledge in the best way to make good choices.
- Wa Alaikum Salaam: The reply to "As-salaamu Alaikum," meaning "Peace be upon you too."
- Wahy: Messages from Allah given to prophets through angels like Jibreel (Gabriel).
- Witr: An odd-numbered prayer offered after the Isha (night) prayer.

- Walima: A marriage banquet or celebration, typically held after the wedding.
- Wajib: Obligatory actions that a Muslim must perform according to Islamic law.
- Wasila: A means of seeking closeness to Allah, especially through prayer or good deeds.
- Worldly Life (Dunya): The material, temporary world in which people live, in contrast to the eternal life in the Hereafter.
- Waqf: A charitable endowment, often in the form of land or property, donated for religious or educational purposes.
- Waqt: Time, often referring to the importance of time in Islam, especially in relation to prayers and good deeds.

X

- Xenophobia: A big word for being afraid of people who are different. Islam teaches us to love and respect everyone!
- X-Ray of the Heart: A way to think about how Allah knows everything in our hearts, even if no one else sees.

Y

- Yaseen: A special chapter in the Quran, often called the heart of the Quran.

- Yawm-ul-Qiyamah: The Day of Judgment when everyone will meet Allah.
- Yusuf (Joseph): A prophet known for his beauty, wisdom, and patience.
- Yaqeen: A strong belief and trust in Allah, no matter what happens.
- Yaseer: A name meaning "easy" or "gentle," sometimes used to refer to the ease of the Quran or life.
- Yaqin: Absolute certainty, a deep and unshakeable belief in the truth of Allah's teachings.
- Yazid: A name that can refer to historical figures, including the controversial caliph Yazid ibn Muawiya.

- Yawm al-Mawt: The Day of Death, the day when every soul will leave the body.
- Yunus (Jonah): A prophet who was swallowed by a big fish and later freed after repenting.
- Yahya (John): The name of a prophet, known for his righteousness and devotion to Allah.
- Yad: Means "hand" in Arabic, often used symbolically for power, strength, or authority.
- Yusuf's Shirt: A symbol of forgiveness, associated with the story of Prophet Yusuf and his reunion with his father Ya'qub.
- Yarmouk: The site of a famous battle in Islamic history between the Byzantine Empire and the Rashidun Caliphate.
- Yamin: Meaning "right" or "right-hand," it can also refer to a pledge or oath in Islamic tradition.
- Yahudi: A term used for Jews, in reference to the followers of the Abrahamic faith.

Z

- Zakat: Giving a part of your money to help people in need.

- Zamzam: A special well in Makkah with blessed water that never runs out.
- Zikr: Remembering Allah by saying His names and praising Him.
- Zuhd: Living simply and focusing on Allah instead of loving too many worldly things.
- Zabur: The holy book revealed to Prophet Dawood (David).
- Zakat al-Fitr: A form of charity given at the end of Ramadan to purify fasting.
- Zamzam Water: Sacred water from the Zamzam well in Makkah, believed to be blessed.
- Zawiya: A Sufi lodge or place for spiritual retreat and worship.
- Zina: Forbidden sexual relations outside of marriage.
- Zindiq: A term historically used for heretics or those accused of holding unorthodox views.

- Zubur: Refers to the Psalms of David (Dawood), one of the holy books in Islam.
- Zaidiyyah: A sect within Shia Islam, particularly in Yemen, that follows the teachings of Zayd ibn Ali.
- Zakat al-Mal: The annual obligatory almsgiving of a portion of wealth to those in need.
- Zikr al-Jami': A comprehensive form of remembering Allah that encompasses both physical and verbal acts.
- Zulfiqar: The famous sword of Imam Ali, known for its unique and distinctive shape.

www.ingramcontent.com/pod-product-compliance
Lightning Source LLC
LaVergne TN
LVHW070049070526
838201LV00040B/410